W9-AHA-141

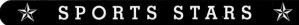
MARIO LEMIEUX

SUPER MARIO

By Ted Cox

CHILDRENS PRESS ®
CHICAGO

Photo Credits

Cover, Allsport USA; 6, UPI/Bettmann; 9, 10, AP/Wide World; 13, UPI/
Bettmann; 15, Reuters/Bettmann; 17, 18, UPI/Bettmann; 21, Bruce
Bennett/© B. Bennett Studios; 22, Reuters/Bettmann; 24, 25, UPI/
Bettmann; 27, Focus On Sports; 28, J. Giamundo/©B. Bennett Studios;
31, ©David Klutho/Allsport USA; 32, 33, 34, Reuters/Bettmann; 37,
Allsport USA; 38, 39, Reuters/Bettmann; 41, AP/Wide World; 42, Michael
DiGirolamo/©B. Bennett Studios; 47, Bruce Bennett/©B. Bennett Studios

Project Editor: Shari Joffe
Design: Beth Herman Design Associates
Photo Research: Jan Izzo

Library of Congress Cataloging-in-Publication Data

Cox, Ted.
    Mario Lemieux (super Mario) / by Ted Cox.
        p. cm.–(Sports stars)
    Summary: A biography of Mario Lemieux, detailing his career as
a hockey superstar with the Pittsburgh Penguins.
        ISBN 0-516-04378-1
        1. Lemieux, Mario, 1965- –Juvenile literature. 2. Hockey players–
Canada–Biography–Juvenile literature. [1. Lemieux, Mario, 1965- .
2. Hockey players.] I. Title. II. Series.
GV850.L45C69   1993
796.962'092–dc20   93-19782
[B]   CIP
                                                                    AC

MARIO LEMIEUX

SUPER MARIO

From the time he was a teenager playing junior hockey, Mario Lemieux was expected to be great. He was big. He was a fast skater. He could shoot and pass the puck like no one else his age.

The question was, how great would he be? Would he make it to the National Hockey League? Would he be an All-Star? Would he win the Stanley Cup?

Mario Lemieux made the NHL. He became an All-Star and the best hockey player in the world. A back injury almost ended his career. But he came back to win the Stanley Cup two years in a row. Then he found out there was even more to being a champion than scoring goals and winning games.

Mario Lemieux was born on October 5, 1965, in Montreal, Quebec, to French-Canadian parents. His family name is pronounced "le myoo." In French that means "the best." It wasn't long before Mario started living up to his name.

Mario was the youngest of three brothers. His dad, Jean-Guy, was a construction worker. His mom, Pierette, stayed home and raised the three boys. The Lemieuxs encouraged their sons to play hockey, Canada's national sport. "I started to skate when I was two or three, and played my first game at six," Mario said. "By the time I was twelve, I knew I had a lot of talent."

Richard, the oldest, was a good player, but Alain, the middle brother, was better. In Canada, the top prospects play junior hockey when they are teenagers. Alain played for a team in Laval, a suburb of Montreal. Mario followed him to Laval when he was sixteen. Mario soon showed he was even better than his brothers. Within two years, he was the best player in the league. In 1983-84, he scored 133 goals and assisted on 149 of his teammates' goals. He averaged nearly two goals and more than four points a game.

Mario tries to control the puck through a maze of sticks.

Mario reacts to scoring his first NHL goal.

The NHL draft allows the worst team to pick the best young player. The Pittsburgh Penguins had joined the league in 1967, but they had never been very good. In 1984, they were the worst team in the league. They picked Mario.

Mario was nervous before his first game, against the Boston Bruins. But in his first shift on the ice, he stole the puck from All-Star defenseman Ray Bourque and scored. Mario was on his way.

He scored 43 goals that season and assisted on 57 others. That added up to 100 points. Only two other players had ever reached that level in their rookie season. Mario won the Calder Memorial Trophy, awarded to the player named NHL Rookie of the Year.

Mario was also picked for the All-Star Game. He scored two goals and passed out an assist and was named the game's most valuable player. "It was a great feeling to play in the All-Star Game my first year in the league," he said. "That was my type of game—almost no hitting and a lot of skating and passing."

Hockey is a rough sport because it's played on ice. Players try to knock each other down, using bumps or "checks," in order to steal the puck. Most of the great hockey players have been either big, or fast. Mario was both.

An opponent tries to check Mario, but Mario has already sent
the puck flying.

But he was a long way from being the best in the league. When Mario came up, Wayne Gretzky was the best player in hockey. During Mario's impressive 100-point rookie season, the Great Gretzky scored 208 points and led his Edmonton Oilers to their second straight Stanley Cup.

Mario is 6 feet 4 inches tall and weighs more than 200 pounds. That's big for a hockey player —much bigger than Gretzky. Given his size, Mario could easily knock other players around. However, though he can protect himself when hit, Mario doesn't go throwing his weight around. He prefers to skate and pass. He gets even with other players not by hitting—but by scoring goals.

Mario (left) and Wayne Gretzky

That's also the kind of game Gretzky played. But All-Star defenseman Paul Coffey, who played with both Gretzky and Mario, noted an important difference between the two. "Wayne is always looking to pass to set up a goal," he said. "But Mario is capable of going through three or four players to score himself if he wants."

"Before I get the puck," Mario said, "I look where the players are and try to determine where they will be later. I try to get a crowd to go after me, then pass to who's open. It's easy."

Playing hockey was the easy part. Living in a new country was hard. Mario was only nineteen when he came to Pittsburgh, and he didn't speak English. "I used to run into the bathroom after games so I wouldn't have to talk to reporters," he said. He tried to learn by watching lots of television. He especially liked soap operas.

Mario receives a pass from teammate Jim Johnson, who has been knocked into the air by an opponent.

Mario shoots the puck through the back door during a
1987 game.

★ ★ ★

The Penguins arranged for Mario to live with an American family his first season. Tom and Nancy Mathews lived in Pittsburgh and had three boys of their own. They welcomed Mario and made him feel at home. When he moved out, he found a place nearby.

Mario was making good money. His first contract was worth $800,000. He bought his parents, back in Montreal, a satellite dish so they could watch him play on television.

Mario got better and better over the next two years. He scored 54 goals in 1986-87, even though he hurt his knee and missed 17 games.

In September 1987, Mario took part in the
Canada Cup, an international tournament that
brought together the world's best hockey players.
Mario played as a member of Team Canada,
made up of Canadian NHL All-Stars. One of his
teammates was the Great Gretzky. Mario learned
a lot watching the Great One play everyday.
Gretzky always worked hard and tried to do
something amazing every time he stepped on
the ice. In the finals, Team Canada faced the
team from the Soviet Union. Mario scored the
game-winning goal in the final game on a pass
from Gretzky.

In the 1987 Canada Cup, Mario scored the tournament-winning goal on a pass from Gretzky.

In 1988, Mario won both the Hart Memorial Trophy and the Art
Ross Trophy.

Mario returned to Pittsburgh a mature player. In 1987-88, he scored 70 goals to lead the league. He assisted on 98 other goals. This total of 168 points was the most earned by any player that season. Mario won the Art Ross Trophy as the league's leading scorer. He also received the Hart Trophy, awarded to the most valuable player of the regular season. Gretzky had won both those trophies for seven straight seasons before Mario broke his streak.

The Penguins, too, were getting better. But they weren't yet good enough. They had a winning record for the first time in nine years. But they were in the tough Patrick Division, and still finished the season last in the division.

During the 1988-89 season, Mario came into his own. He was twenty-three years old. On New Year's Eve, 1988, he scored five goals in one game against the New Jersey Devils.

Mario celebrates a goal during an NHL All-Star Game.

Mario went on to lead the league in goals that season, with 85. He tied Gretzky for the lead in assists, with 114. His 199 points won him a second straight Art Ross Trophy as the league's leading scorer. He set a record by earning six points in the All-Star Game. And, best of all, the Penguins made the playoffs.

They had won half of their 80 regular-season games, allowing them to finish second in their division. They swept their first playoff series and went up against the Philadelphia Flyers.

The two teams split the first four games of the best-of-seven series. Mario had injured his neck and nearly didn't play the fifth game. But he did play, and blitzed the Flyers with four goals in the

Mario prepares to score during a 1989 playoff game.

first period. He scored another into an empty net at the end of the game. He tied five Stanley Cup records with his five goals and three assists. "He took control of the game the way only Mario can," said the Pens' Bob Errey. "I don't know if I've ever seen him better."

The Penguins led the series 3-2, but the Flyers were determined to stop Mario. They followed him everywhere the next two games and came back to eliminate the Penguins.

Mario couldn't be too disappointed. He had established himself on the ice, and he was settled in his new hometown. He was named Pittsburgh's man of the year. His salary was now almost $2 million. He built a big house outside the city for himself and Nathalie Asselin, his sweetheart from Montreal.

Pittsburgh has become Mario's adopted home.

"I want to live here," Mario said. "Pittsburgh is so much different from Montreal. Montreal is a big, big city. Here you can walk the streets at night and nobody bothers you."

Mario had also learned to become a leader. He was now the team's captain. He led by example, but he was also known to crack up his teammates with imitations of Elvis Presley and Pee Wee Herman.

The next year was his best—and his worst.
In November 1989, he began a scoring streak.
In every game, he either scored a goal or earned
an assist. Gretzky held the scoring-streak record,
at 51 straight games. Mario's streak was the talk
of the All-Star break in January. Fans began
calling him "Super Mario" after the video-game
character. Mario shook off the pressure to set a
record with four goals in the All-Star Game. But
his back was hurting. The pain wouldn't go away.

The streak was at 46 on February 14. But
Mario felt awful. He tried to play, but the pain
was too much. He couldn't even leave the locker
room for the final period. The streak was over.

So was Mario's season. He played very little
after that. Without Mario, the Penguins failed
to make the playoffs.

Mario had a herniated disk in his back. He needed an operation. It was possible he might never play again. He got an infection in his back after the operation. He missed more than half of the 1990-91 season. But he came back, and when he did, he found his teammates were better. Over the years, the team had added stars like defenseman Paul Coffey, left wing Kevin Stevens, and goalie Tom Barrasso. In 1990-91, they added a young player from Czechoslovakia named Jaromir Jagr. He was 6 feet 2 inches tall and 200 pounds, a good skater with good moves. People began calling him "Little Mario."

With Mario back, the Penguins finished first and went into the playoffs hot. They won their division playoffs and the conference finals. They would play the Minnesota North Stars for the Stanley Cup.

Mario and a St. Louis player battle for the puck.

Minnesota took a 2-1 lead when Mario
missed the third game with back spasms. Mario
returned to score three early goals in the fourth
game and tie the series. At the start of the next
game, Minnesota's Brian Flynn ran into Mario
with his stick. The referees called a penalty for
cross-checking. With Flynn in the penalty box,
Mario made them pay right away. He scored
on the power play and led the Penguins to
another win.

Mario scores a goal during the 1991 Stanley Cup Finals.

The Penguins were one game away from the Stanley Cup. Mario and his teammates were ready. Mario scored a goal and assisted on three others as the Penguins won by an 8-0 shutout. They were world champions.

On the way to victory in the 1991 Stanley Cup Finals

Hoisting the 1991 Stanley Cup for all to see

Mario hoisted the Stanley Cup for all the fans and his teammates to see. "It was no strain on my back to lift it," he joked afterward.

Mario won the Conn Smythe Trophy, awarded to the most valuable player of the Stanley Cup Playoffs. He had scored 44 points in the 23 playoff games. Only Gretzky had scored more: 47 in 1985.

Mario credited his coach, Bob Johnson. "He made us believe we could win the Cup," he said. But the Penguins didn't know their coach was very sick. He had brain cancer. Johnson died that November.

The Penguins were rattled at the start of the 1991-92 season. They had a tough time adjusting to new coach Scotty Bowman. They made the playoffs, but finished third in their division. Mario missed a few regular-season games with back problems, but piled up a league-leading 131 points to win his third Art Ross Trophy.

In the playoffs, the Penguins started slow, but won their first series. They advanced to play the Rangers in the division finals. They won the first game. But in the second game, New York's Adam Graves chopped Mario on the hand with his stick. It broke a bone. The Penguins would have to get past the Rangers without Mario if they wanted him to return for the conference finals.

They did. The Penguins beat the Rangers in six games. With Mario coming back, the Pens were confident against the Bruins in the conference finals. Mario returned in the second game as the Penguins swept the series.

The Penguins faced the Chicago Blackhawks in the Stanley Cup finals. The Hawks took a 4-1 lead in the first game. But the Penguins rebounded. Jagr scored the tying goal in the third period. Then Mario won it with a goal in the final minute. It was the greatest comeback in the Stanley Cup Finals since 1944.

When on the ice, Mario always gives it his all.

The Hawks never recovered. The Penguins swept the series. Mario was named the playoff MVP for the second straight year. Not even Gretzky had done that.

Blackhawks coach Mike Keenan said that Mario and Jagr were the two best players in the world. People started talking about a Pittsburgh dynasty. "Dynasty, that's a pretty strong word," said Mario. "But I like our chances the next few years with Jagr coming up."

Mario and teammates Rick Tocchet, Jaromir Jagr, and Bryan Trottier celebrate their second straight Stanley Cup.

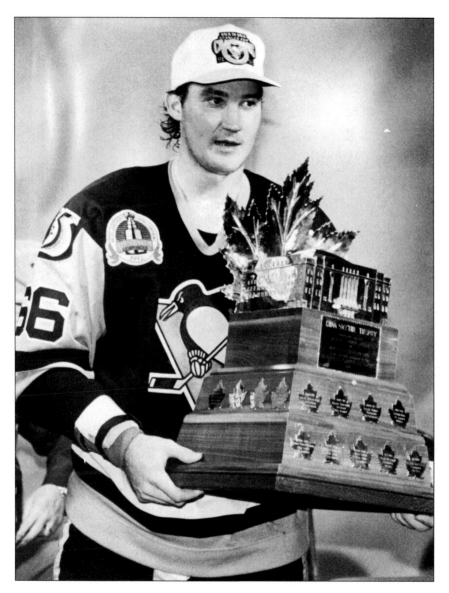

Mario was named playoff MVP for the second straight year in 1992.

When the 1992-93 season started, the Penguins set out to show just how good they could be. At the All-Star break, the Penguins had the best record in the league. And Mario had 104 points halfway through the season. He had a chance to break Gretzky's record of 215 points.

But Mario wasn't feeling well again. In January 1993, doctors found a lump on his neck and discovered he had a mild form of cancer called Hodgkin's disease. Doctors treat Hodgkin's disease with radiation treatments, and most patients recover completely. But the treatments would be hard on Mario's body. They would make him tired and weak. He would have to leave the team until they were over.

"I've faced a lot of battles since I was really young, and I've always come out on top," Mario said. "I expect that will be the case with this disease.

"I'll be back when I'm 100-percent cured,"
he added. "Hopefully, that will be in time for the
playoffs, and I can help us win another Stanley
Cup. But first things first."

On March 2, 1993, just hours after he received
his last radiation treatment, Mario flew to
Philadelphia and dressed for a game against the
Flyers. When he skated onto the ice that night,
the fans welcomed him with a standing ovation.
During the game, the remarkable Mario scored
a goal and assisted on another.

While Mario was out, Pat LaFontaine of the Buffalo Sabres had seized the league lead in scoring. Mario charged from behind. He wasn't yet back to full strength, but he was playing his best hockey. He scored five goals in one game and caught LaFontaine at the end of the season, winning the Art Ross trophy going away. LaFontaine played all 84 games and finished with 148 points. Mario played in only 60 games, but finished with 69 goals, 91 assists, and 160 points. There was no longer any doubt about who was hockey's greatest player.

The Penguins finished the season with the best record in the league, but they couldn't win their third straight Stanley Cup. They were upset by the New York Islanders in a tough, seven-game series in the division finals. But after all he had gone through, it was a relatively minor setback for Mario. He and the Penguins would find a way to come back. Mario always has.

Chronology

1965 – Mario Lemieux is born October 5 in Montreal, Quebec, Canada.

1981 – Mario joins the Laval team in the Quebec Major Junior Hockey League (QMJHL).

1984 – Mario is named the QMJHL's most valuable player after leading the league with 133 goals, 149 assists, and 282 points in 70 games in the regular season. In the playoffs, he leads all players with 29 goals, 23 assists, and 52 points.
– Mario is chosen by the Pittsburgh Penguins as the first player picked in the National Hockey League draft.

1985 – Mario finishes the regular season with 43 goals and 57 assists for 100 points.
– In the All–Star Game, Mario scores two goals, adds an assist, and is named MVP of the game.
– Mario is named NHL Rookie of the Year.

1987 – Mario reaches the 50–goal plateau for the first time and finishes the season with 54.
– Mario plays with Team Canada in the Canada Cup, and scores the game–winning goal in the last game of the finals against the Soviet Union.

1988 – Mario leads the NHL with 70 goals and 168 points, earning the Art Ross Memorial Trophy as the league's leading scorer. He wins the Hart Memorial Trophy as the regular–season MVP.

1989 – Mario leads the league with 85 goals and ties Wayne Gretzky for the lead in assists with 114. His 199 points give him his second straight Art Ross Trophy.
   – Mario scores 12 points in 11 games as the Penguins advance to the division finals of the Stanley Cup Playoffs.

1990 – Mario puts together a 46–game scoring streak, but a herniated disk ends his season.
   – Mario undergoes an operation on his back. An infection prolongs his recovery period.

1991 – Mario returns to the lineup and leads the Penguins to first place in the Patrick Division.
   – In the playoffs, Mario leads all players with 28 assists and 44 points.
   – The Penguins win the Stanley Cup Finals 4–2 over the Minnesota North Stars. Mario wins the Conn Smythe Trophy as the most valuable player in the playoffs.

1992– Mario leads the league with 131 points to claim his third
Art Ross Trophy.
– Mario is injured in the division playoffs with a broken
hand and misses six games. He returns in time to lead
the Penguins to their second straight Stanley Cup with
a series sweep of the Chicago Blackhawks. Having led
all players with 16 goals and 34 points in the playoffs,
Mario wins his second straight Conn Smythe Trophy.

1993 – Mario is diagnosed with Hodgkin's Disease in January
and undergoes radiation treatments.
– Two months later, Mario returns to the ice. He leads the
Penguins to first place with the best record in the NHL,
and he recaptures the lead in the scoring race, in spite
of missing 24 games of the season.
– Mario wins his fourth Art Ross Trophy with 69 goals,
91 assists, and 160 points. The Penguins are eliminated
in the division finals, but after the season, Mario claims
his second Hart Memorial Trophy as the league's MVP.

★ ★ ★

About the Author

Ted Cox is a Chicago journalist who works at the *Daily Southtown*. He has covered sports for the Chicago *Reader* and *Chicago* magazine. He worked at United Press International and holds a B.S. in journalism from the University of Illinois at Urbana-Champaign. He lives in Chicago with his wife, Catherine, and their daughter, Sadie.